# Kama Sutra

# Kama Sutra

## THE ARTS OF LOVE

**Thorsons**
*An Imprint of* HarperCollins*Publishers*

The publishers wish to emphasise that they are not
responsible for any injury to any persons caused by
attempting any of the positions described here.

Thorsons
An Imprint of HarperCollins*Publishers*
77-85 Fulham Palace Road,
Hammersmith, London W6 8JB
&
1160 Battery Street,
San Francisco, California 94111-1213

Published by Thorsons 1992
in association with Vision Video Ltd.

© Norse Music Productions Ltd. 1992
Photographs © Adam Tysoe 1992

Text: Indra Sinha, Zek Halu, Misha Halu
Editor: Jane Graham-Maw
Designer: Rosamund Saunders

Grateful acknowledgement is made to
Nicholas Enterprises Ltd.
for permission to reproduce extracts from
*Love Teachings of Kama Sutra* translated by Indra Sinha
and published in Great Britain by
the Hamlyn Publishing Group Ltd.,
denoted in the text by use of "double quotes".

A catalogue record for this book
is available from the British Library

ISBN 0 7225 2837X

Typeset in Weiss

Printed in the U.S.A.

"Woman is the sacrificial fire,
 the lips of her yoni the fuel
 the hairs around them the smoke
 and her love temple itself the flame.

"The act of entry is the kindling
 the blaze of pleasure is the sparks.
 In this fire the gods offer up seed grain
 of which sacred offering, man is born."

*After reading and considering the works of Babhravya and other ancient authors, and thinking over the meaning of the rules given by them, this treatise was composed, according to the precepts of the Holy Writ, for the benefit of the world, by Vatsyayana, while leading the life of a religious student at Benares, and wholly engaged in the contemplation of the Deity.*

The *Kama Sutra* is the most famous book on lovemaking ever written. Originally composed by an Indian sage sometime between the fourth century BC and the first century AD, it was not translated into English until the 1880s, and has only been available to the general reader since the 1960s.

Not much is known about the author of the *Kama Sutra*. He belonged to the Vatsyayana sept, and his own name was Mallanaga. He embarked on the book as he was nearing the end of his life, and saw the writing of it as part of his religious duties. It is a learned and carefully researched work, objective and semi-scientific, and is itself based on the writings of earlier sages.

The *Kama Sutra* was written at a time when a cultured Hindu was expected to acquire three 'principles': *Dharma*, or religious merit, *Artha*, or worldly wealth, and *Kama*, the science of love and pleasure. Vatsyayana emphasises that 'this work is not to be used merely as an instrument for satisfying our desires.' However, it became, over the years, an essential part of the reading of thousands of Indians, and unlike other authors who wrote exclusively for men, Vatsyayana's classic book was used to instruct young brides before their weddings.

We owe much to the Victorian scholar and explorer Richard Burton and his associate Foster Arbuthnot, who took great pains to translate the original Sanskrit.

In the face of opposition and risking prosecution, they published it in 1883 under the fictitious imprint *The Kama Shastra Society of London and Benares*. It was circulated, with other translations of Eastern texts such as *The Perfumed Garden*, the *Ananga Ranga* and *The Arabian Nights*, among an elite group of people who were interested in the customs and behaviour of the Orient, although undoubtedly it was also used as a manual for Victorian husbands. Since it was discovered, the *Kama Sutra* revolutionised the Western approach to Indian culture, showing as it does how central and natural sex was to Indian thought.

The Sanskrit term *Kama* meant 'love, pleasure, sensual gratification', while *Sutra* meant 'aphorisms, compressed expressions' – a way of expressing complicated doctrines often used in early Sanskrit texts. But Kama is far more than just erotic pleasure. It encompasses all sensory pleasures. Thus good food, silken clothes, perfumes, music and painting all came within Kama's realm. When Vatsyayana named his treatise 'Kama Sutra', he intended to lay down ideals for the enjoyment of all these pleasures. So he describes how the house of the ideal citizen is to be built, furnished and provisioned. Which sweet scented flowers should be grown in the gardens. With which paintings and sculptures the rooms should be adorned, what incenses should perfume the air and what music should attend the meetings of lovers.

In a very real sense, sex was considered by the Hindus not only natural and necessary, but almost sacramental – the human counterpart of the miracle of creation. Erotic statues and carvings all over India testify to the fact that it was a subject to be approached with reverence and objectivity, rather than as something obscene and secret.

The *Kama Sutra* in its entirety is a long work, and consists not only of detailed advice on the sexual act itself – in the section of the book known as 'the 64' – but also lays down instructions on courtship, marriage, education, household management, medicine, and various accomplishments cultured men and women needed to acquire in order to attract the opposite sex. Other chapters, such as those on prostitutes and courtesans, ritualised violence, the seduction of virgins and other men's wives, the use of go-betweens and harems, and the inherent racism and sexism, strike us today as irrelevant and, in parts, morally unacceptable. Taken as a whole, though, they give a fascinating picture of a dead civilisation – a formalised world of pleasure-gardens and palaces, of beautiful scented women, hedonistic courtiers and irrational, polygamous kings. A world, moreover, in which sexual expertise was elevated to a high art.

In India the *Kama Sutra* is still regarded as being of contemporary value, because its essence is not pleasure that comes from outside. It is about the

*"Kama is the breath of lip on lip, the
caress of breasts, hips, buttocks,
thighs, in the beautiful embrace from
which a child is born: learn it from
Kama Sutra and the world."*

enjoyment that comes from within – the pleasure to be had from two bodies and minds.

The *Kama Sutra* introduces us to a wide variety of sexual techniques and lovemaking positions, or 'asanas'. Some demand a fairly high degree of acrobatic ingenuity, and others require a flexibility that our rigid Western bodies are not used to, so please do take care. We have inevitably had to be selective in the positions we have chosen to illustrate here, but we are confident that those pictured will provide a wonderfully varied and exciting way into the mysteries of the *Kama Sutra*. For the positions not illustrated here we have included sections from Burton's translation and from the Arab classic *The Perfumed Garden*, which

was written in a quite different style but nevertheless gives details of many exotic and fascinating postures.

The *Kama Sutra* is not pornography, nor is it a sex manual. It is a work of art, making skilful use of the Sanskrit language to convey different levels of meaning, both practical and philosophical, physical and metaphysical. It is as much about the spiritual side of love and sex as it is about exploring new erotic possibilities. The writer of the *Kama Sutra* knew something that we have perhaps forgotten: that the sexual union of two people is an event far more profound than just pleasure-seeking. Again and again in the terse Sanskrit stanzas of the *Kama Sutra*, we encounter hints and clues of something deeper.

The text for this edition is a blend of three elements. Excerpts from Burton's translation give a flavour of the formality and aphoristic nature of the original, while free verse extracts translated by the scholar and writer Indra Sinha in 1980 convey the poetic and sensuous spirit of Vatsyayana's classic work. The explanatory text is adapted from the script of the Vision video, a collaboration between Indra Sinha and Zek and Misha Halu, sex therapists, healers and specialists in ancient oriental sexual arts.

Although the focus is on heterosexual relationships, many of the general recommendations apply equally to gay and lesbian relationships. Furthermore, with the prevalence of AIDS and other sexually transmitted diseases you are risking your life, and your partner's life, if you do not practise safe sex. This book is designed to be used as an adjunct to a loving, monogamous relationship.

Nearly two thousand years ago, in an Indian city halfway across the world, an old man sat down to write a book. He began by telling a story that was already thousands of years old, even in his day.

The great god Shiva, terrible destroyer of worlds, the ultimate teacher of all yoga, meditation and magic, was in the mood for love. Shiva and his wife, the beautiful goddess Parvati, locked themselves away in their room in their palace on Mount Kailash.

A year passed, and another, and the divine couple did not emerge. Ten thousand years went by and still they remained secluded. Only Nandi, the white bull, on guard outside the doors of their room, knew what was happening within.

What was happening was lovemaking of a kind that most human beings will never experience. Lovemaking that annihilates time. Of these things, Nandi was sworn never to speak.

But he could not help himself. What he had overheard was so overwhelming that it could by no means be kept secret.

But even as Nandi broke his vow and spoke, the words turned to flowers that dropped from his mouth. These flowers were collected together and strung on threads, and wise men meditating upon them composed the first ever texts on lovemaking.

This first book was so huge that it would have made even the mighty *Decline and Fall of the Roman Empire* look like a footnote. So it was abbreviated. Once, then twice, then many times more. Teams of sages, working over a thousand years, condensed and condensed the sacred love teachings.

At last, at a time when the Roman empire was indeed hastening to decline, the entire Indian love tradition was distilled into a mere 4,000 stanzas – by one Mallanaga Vatsyayana.

He called his book *Kama Sutra*.

*Kama Sutra*, the Arts of Love. It remains to this day, the most famous – and the most potent – work on lovemaking ever written.

Vatsyayana's world, situated in the India of, probably, the fourth century AD, could hardly be more

different from ours. It was a world of arrogant kings and chariot armies, of beauties locked in harems, of rich urban playboys and skilled courtesans. But although music, drama and art all reached new heights in this era, many of its social attitudes strike us today as unacceptable.

So what is it that still lures us? After all, there are plenty of modern lovemaking manuals – why do we still turn with such fascination to a book written nearly two thousand years ago?

Perhaps because the subjects it deals with – love, sex, the body – are as relevant to us today as the day Vatsyayana first put pen to paper.

After all, the human body has not changed in the last two millennia. Nor the human emotions, love, fear, pleasure, anger and desire. Lovemaking is the only human activity that can transcend all cultures, all ages, all philosophies and all manners.

This book shows couples making love in some of the postures advocated by the *Kama Sutra*. But don't be fooled into thinking that it's the postures that are important. They're not. On its own, each posture is as meaningless as a single note of music – its value in a piece of music is determined by its relationship to other notes that come before and after.

Lovemaking should flow like music, one position changing easily and effortlessly to the next. To do this takes practice. You don't need to use every technique

illustrated here; nor is it the physical performance that's really important. What matters is the feelings that we put into our lovemaking. Every action, every sound, every caress, every part of our body should express our affection, our tenderness, our loving care for our partner.

The mind is the most powerful sex organ of all. The forever-shifting, changing postures, flowing like dance figures from one to another, are expressions of the tenderness of the controlling mind. And for this reason, the *Kama Sutra* is especially valuable to couples who are married, or who are committed to each other in a long-term relationship.

Vatsyayana wrote that, properly practised, the arts of his *Kama Sutra* are so powerful that the love they arouse will not diminish, even in a thousand years.

*"Let your house for seven days and nights,*
*be filled with singing;*
*set musicians behind carved screens*
*to play as you bathe together."*

A bath taken together is one of the best ways to begin a lovemaking session. It allows you to touch each other's bodies with affection rather than passion. Passion comes later. It permits you to play games.

*Kama* is often translated as desire. But it is far more than just sexual pleasure.

*Kama* is all sensual pleasures, the delight of all five senses, of sight and sound, of touch and taste and smell.

*Kama* is the delight of seeing your lover's body. The smell of his, or her, hair. The delicious sensation of skin touching skin.

Ask the question, 'What is lovemaking?' and many people will immediately think of intercourse. But real sex, the lovemaking taught by the ancient texts, begins long before even arousal.

Lovemaking is the time spent just being together. Walking, talking or meditating. Sitting reading in the same room, or to one another. Singing together. And, of course, caring for one another's bodies.

It is above all expressing feelings of affection and care. When you touch one another's bodies, pay attention to what you are doing, be aware of every little action. One of the great secrets of lovemaking is this: slow down. Whatever you are doing, it will be better at half the speed.

Nothing heightens desire like expectation. Let your every touch contain a new idea, and let each contact burn like a cool fire.

In the bath, you may tease and tantalize, building an appetite for the more intense pleasure to come.

Embracing and making love in the water is called VARIKRIDA – the Water Game.

The embrace which indicates the mutual love of a man
and woman who have come together is of four kinds:

Touching — Piercing — Rubbing — Pressing

The action in each case is denoted by the meaning of
the word which stands for it.

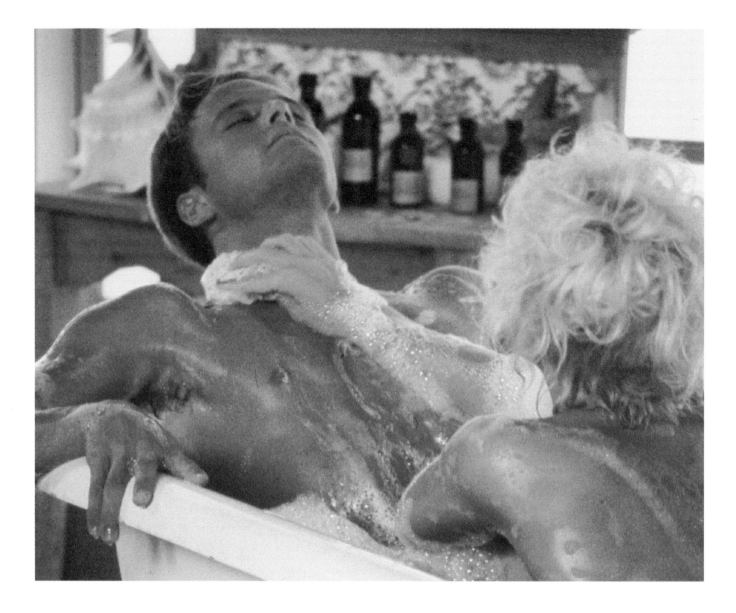

"There are very many lovely caresses which have
never been mentioned in the love teachings…
It's for you to discover them with your lover
and use them whenever you can
for they will sharpen both pleasure and desire."

As with caresses, so with kisses. Not all kisses need to be deep, French kisses. In the early stages of love-making, it is better to nibble and nuzzle.

When washing one another it would be perfectly
possible to do it quickly and mechanically, without
feeling. But when you put your feeling into it, you
can be infinitely tender.

When a man under some pretext or other goes in front of or alongside a woman and touches her body with his own, it is called the 'touching embrace'.

When a woman in a lonely place bends down, as if to pick up something, and pierces, as it were, a man sitting or standing, with her breasts, and the man in return takes hold of them, it is called a 'piercing embrace'.

The above two kinds of embrace take place only between persons who do not, as yet, speak freely with each other.

When two lovers are walking slowly together, either in the dark, or a place of public resort, or in a lonely place, and rub their bodies against each other, it is called a 'rubbing embrace'

When on the above occasion one of them presses the other's body forcibly against a wall or pillar, it is called a 'pressing embrace'.

These last two are peculiar to those who know the intentions of each other.

*When both the man and the woman afford mutual
pleasure to each other. . . such is called a connection in
the proper sense of the word.*

Suvarnanabha says that while a man is doing to the woman what he likes best during congress, he should always make a point of pressing those parts of her body on which she turns her eyes.

His hand travels down to between her legs
where the towel is rubbed gently. Many couples
only touch each other's most intimate parts during or
just before sex. It is important to learn to touch each
other easily and without embarrassment, even
without the lights out.

The roughness of a towel on smooth
skin can be very invigorating, toning
and stimulating the skin. Creating
exquisite sensations…

…which are as every bit as delicious
in their own right as the pleasures
which are to follow.

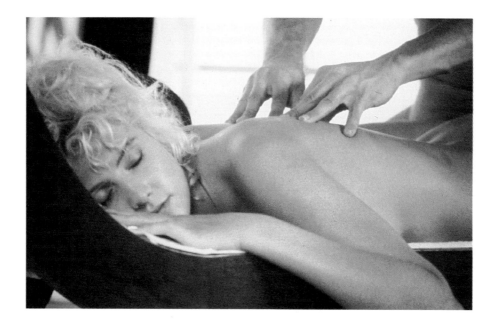

*"Give her your jasmine garland*
*lie her gently back and massage her body*
*with sweet sandal-oil."*

Having bathed, your bodies are clean and sweet-scented, refreshed and relaxed. Even though you may be ready for making love, be patient just a little longer. You have still hardly begun to experience the pleasure that Kama has in store for you.

In Vatsyayana's day, they were as fond as we are today of exotic perfumes. Then, as now, it was an exquisite pleasure to be massaged with fragrant oils, such as jasmine, sandalwood, musk, ylang ylang, bergamot and thyme.

The simplest form of massage is just rubbing in the scented oils to your lover's skin. If you are prepared to learn, there are many different styles of massage, many of which are very beneficial to health. And, of course, sex will be so much better when every muscle is relaxed.

The art of enjoying Kama is to be able to recognise and experience to the full all the many different sorts of pleasure.

Those who become lovers of extreme skill never forget that the greatest enjoyment is the pleasure of caring for one another.

He rubs both of his hands up and down her back, over her buttocks and along the backs of her legs. She does not lie passively, but lifts her feet up behind her as he oils them.

Sitting astride him, her hands play up and down his chest, cupping his pectoral muscles, flattening them and repeating. Whatever the form of massage you practise, try to keep it non-sexual for as long as you can.

*In the pleasure room, decorated with flowers, and fragrant with perfumes...the citizen should receive the woman, who will come bathed and dressed, and should invite her to take refreshment and to drink freely. He should then seat her on his left side, and holding her hair, and touching also the end and knot of her garment, he should gently embrace her with his right arm. They should then carry on an amusing conversation on various subjects, and may also talk suggestively of things which would be considered as coarse, or not to be mentioned generally in society.*

*They may then sing, either with or without gesticulations, and play on musical instruments, talk about the arts, and persuade each other to drink. At last when the woman is overcome with love and desire, and the two are left alone, they should proceed as the Kama Sutra describes.*

Love-making does not, of course, only have to take place in the bedroom, but the *Kama Sutra* teaches that atmosphere is all-important. Use soft cushions and rugs, candles or low lighting to create a warm and intimate environment to relax in, freeing you from cares to explore each other's bodies.

Approaching from behind, he
embraces her and she sinks
luxuriously into his arms.

*"Kama is the delight of body, mind
and soul in exquisite sensation:
awaken eyes, nose, tongue, ears, skin,
and between sense and sensed
the essence of Kama will flower."*

Kissing the exposed nape of her neck, his hand
comes up to rub the other side of her face and
she turns her face to him, turning her body in
the process.

On the occasion of the first congress,
kissing and the other things mentioned
above should be done moderately,
they should not be continued for a
long time, and should be done
alternately. On subsequent occasions,
however, the reverse of all this may
take place, and moderation will not be
necessary, they may continue for a
long time, and for the purpose of
kindling love they may all be done at
the same time.

*The following are the places for
kissing: the forehead, the eyes,
the cheeks, the throat, the bosom,
the breasts, the lips and the interior of
the mouth. Moreover, the people of the
Lat country kiss also the following
places: the joints of the thighs, the
arms and the navel.*

Gathering her face
in both his hands he
cups it and pulls her up
to his lips, kissing it all
over and finally giving
her a 'turned' kiss.
She glides down his
chest, kissing as she
goes, and running her
hands down his back,
sinks to her knees.
He bends down and
kisses her lips, offered
up to him, in the 'bent'
kiss. Thus, while still
kissing, he too sinks to
his knees and, his hands
still on her face,
touches her lips.

His hand gently
squeezes the flesh of
her back.

She straddles one of his thighs as they embrace.
His leg is raised up into her crotch as his hands play
up and down her back. She clasps his head to her
and nuzzles him into her bosom as she clamps his
leg between her own.

Her nails circle around his shoulder blade. Her forefinger can be extended to score a trail down the central trough of his back and linger at the base of his spine.

According to ancient Indian – and Chinese – tradition, the body is a complex of nerve centres called 'chakras'. At the base of the spine an awesome energy lies coiled. It is called Kundalini. It is roused by lovemaking, but its effects go far beyond. The effect of raising energy in the body, the ancients believed, was to fortify one's spiritual, emotional, mental and physical health. To do this, the energy of Kundalini, once aroused, had to be made to flow round from chakra to chakra, energising and vitalising as it went.

Some schools taught that the raising and control of Kundalini was a way to ultimate salvation – to Moksha – or release from the cycle of love and death. Moksha: the same word is used to describe the female orgasm.

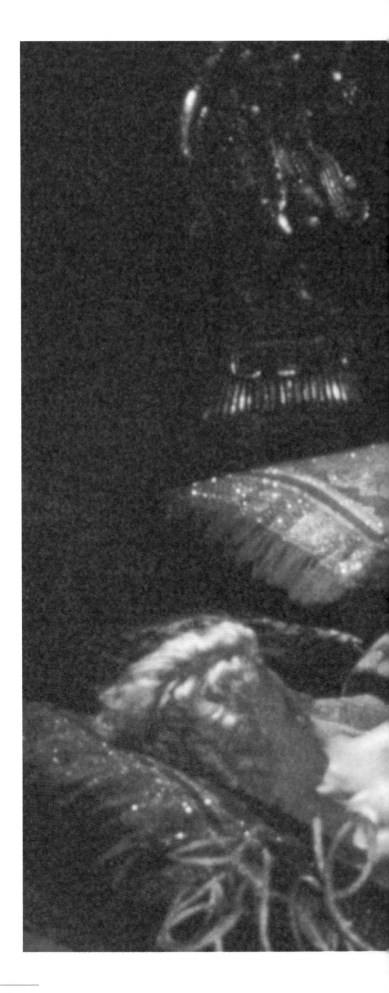

She lies back on the cushions while
his hand gently masturbates her.
Some women like to have an orgasm
before actually making love. The
simplest way to bring her to orgasm
may be to stimulate her clitoris and
vagina with your fingers.

She lies on her back, legs apart and feet lifted well off the cushions.

UTPHALLAKA — the Opening Flower. More usually referred to as the 'missionary' position, this is a good position to start in. It is a beautiful posture, allowing satisfyingly deep penetration and warm, affectionate contact of the upper body.

At last, ready for lovemaking, we come to the postures for which the *Kama Sutra* is famous. Again, remember they are not important in themselves, only as part of an ever-changing dance. The music for this dance is the flow of desire between you. Like dancers, you have to be in control, yet at the same time completely lose yourself in the music.

When the urge to join your bodies becomes overwhelming, then choose a posture to start with and just go with the flow of your feelings.

And from this simple start, see what a lovely
line of postures flows. If she lifts her legs up high,
if necessary steadying her own thighs with her
hands, it becomes VIJRIMBHITAKA — the Widely
Yawning. Even deeper, more intimate penetration
and powerful sensation. Slow, deep strokes of
the penis, more pressing than thrusting,
yield great pleasure.

INDRANI – the position tradition ascribes to the wife of the god Indra, arrived at by a further simple move as she brings her knees to her own shoulders. This posture shortens the vagina and is very intense. The man should be careful not to thrust too hard in case he hurts her, taking his cue from her.

He takes hold of her feet and presses them to her chest, in the most intense of this sequence of postures. It is called RATISUNDARA – Sweet Love – and calls for great skill on the part of the man in the way he uses his penis. Kneeling gives the man tremendous power to vary the depth and direction of his thrusts. In this posture he rotates his hips as he thrusts into her.

This posture is called BHUGNAKA – the Rising.
She lifts her legs up high, keeping them tightly
squeezed together, her knees near his shoulders.
The man now feels the intensity of this posture
sequence, for when she presses her thighs together,
his penis is trapped and deliciously squeezed.

The *Kama Sutra* enumerates many ways that the man
can move his penis in the vagina. Short fluttering
strokes have the strange name of CHATAKAVILASA
– the Sporting of a Sparrow! But deep, circular
motions give the posture variant its name:
SMARACHAKRA – Love's Wheel, which is said to be
a great favourite with passionate women.

PIDITAKA – the Squeeze, intensifies the pressure
as she crosses her raised thighs. This causes a
marvellous sensation which can be made even
more powerful if she now also squeezes with the
muscles of her vagina.

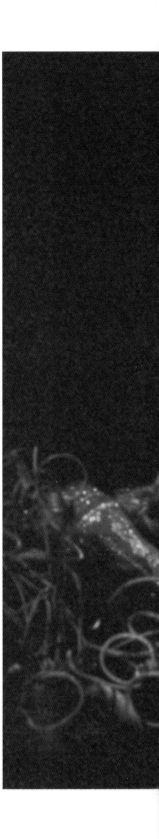

By hooking her feet over his shoulders she opens up
into the deep penetration posture known as
JRIMBHITAKA —the Yawning.

Now she unhooks one leg and stretches it out along
the bed, leaving the other foot on his shoulder. This is
followed by lifting the first leg back and stretching out
the second along the bed, alternationg slowly.

This is the famous VENUDARITAKA — Splitting
the Bamboo. By alternately lowering and stretching
one leg at a time, her vagina rolls and squeezes,
massaging the penis in a most particular way. One of
the great secrets of Indian lovemaking, yet so absurdly
simple when you know how.

While the woman is lying on his bed, and is as it were abstracted by his conversation, he should loosen the knot of her undergarments, and when she begins to dispute with him, he should overwhelm her with kisses. Then when his lingam* is erect he should touch her with his hands in various places, and gently manipulate various parts of the body. If the woman is bashful, and if it is the first time that they have come together, the man should place his hands between her thighs, which she would probably keep close together, and if she is a very young girl, he should first get his hands upon her breasts, which she would probably cover with her own hands, and under her armpits and on her neck.

If however she is a seasoned woman, he should do whatever is agreeable either to him or to her, and whatever is fitting for the occasion. After this he should take hold of her hair, and hold her chin in his fingers for the purpose of kissing her.

* The terms *lingam* and *yoni* are ancient Eastern terms referring to the male and female genitalia respectively.

His finger plays around the mound
of her breast, making the mark of
the Half Moon as it does so.

Who would have thought that
marking with the nails could be
raised to an art? But it can.

*When love becomes intense, pressing
with the nails or scratching the body
with them is practised. It is employed,
together with biting, by those to
whom the practice is agreeable.
Pressing with the nails is of the eight
following kinds, according to the
forms of the marks which are
produced:*

*Sounding – Half Moon – A circle
– A line – A tiger's nail or claw –
A peacock's foot – The jump of a hare
– The leaf of a blue lotus*

*The places that are to be pressed with
the nails are as follows: the armpit, the
throat, the breasts, the lips, the
jaghana, or middle parts of the body,
and the thighs. But Suvarnanabha is
of opinion that when the impetuosity
of passion is excessive, the places need
not be considered…*

*When a person presses the chin, the
breasts, the lower lip, or the jaghana
or another so softly that no scratch or
mark is left, but only the hair on the
body becomes erect from the touch of
the nails, and the nails themselves
make a sound, it is called a 'sounding
or pressing with the nails'.*

Giving names to each nail mark, tooth mark and sexual posture might seem to you to be somewhat unspontaneous. But there was another reason for not giving way – for a long time at least – to unbridled passion.

According to the Indian Tantrics and the Chinese Taoists too, ejaculation was to be avoided in order to prolong lovemaking indefinitely. With practice, they could maintain a near-orgasmic state for hours.

By slowing everything down, when the orgasm finally comes, you may find that you can feel it in every part of your body, from your back and neck to your calves and even the soles of your feet.

*He should gather from the action of*
*the woman what things would be*
*pleasing during congress.*

This embrace, which
allows the woman to
stimulate her clitoris
directly on his thigh,
will prove very erotic
for him too. But let her
take charge, so she can
move whichever way
and at whatever speed
she chooses.

She lies back as he rises to sit on his haunches over
her thighs, reaching forward with his right hand
to her breasts, his left hand anchored on the bottom
of her navel.

He moves down her body, kissing her breasts, navel
and hips. During such long lovemaking, a woman
can enjoy orgasm after orgasm. Many men derive
great pleasure themselves from using their tongues
and lips to bring their lovers to orgasm.

At the first time of sexual union the passion of the
male is intense, and his time is short, but in subsequent
unions on the same day the reverse of this is the case.
With the female however it is the contrary, for at
the first time her passion is weak, and then her time
long, but on subsequent occasions on the same day,
her passion is intense and her time short, until her
passion is satisfied.

*"Place your lover on a couch, set her feet to your
shoulders, clasp her waist, suck hard and let your
tongue stir her overflowing love-temple: this is called
BAHUCHUSHITA — Sucked Hard."*

A medieval Sanskrit text, RATIRATNAPRADIPIKA, which has never been translated into English, gives the eight ancient Indian techniques of cunnilingus. These include licking of the clitoris with the tongue – up and down the clitoris hood, in tiny circles, probing deeply with the tongue into the vagina. By sucking up her inner lips and clitoris into his mouth a man can create exquisite sensations for a woman. You can suck hard and perhaps even nip a little, but with very great care since the clitoris is very sensitive. With all these techniques it is important to find out what she likes and dislikes.

When one of her legs is placed on the head, and the other is stretched out, it is called 'fixing of a nail'. This is learnt by practice only.

When both the legs of the woman are contracted, and placed on her stomach, it is called the 'crab's position'.

When the thighs are raised and placed one upon the other, it is called the 'packed position'.

When the shanks are placed one upon the other, it is called the 'lotus-like position'.

When you are both well aroused and ready, then perhaps try this slightly more advanced sequence of postures:

A man should gather from the actions of the
woman of what disposition she is, and in what
way she likes to be enjoyed.

RATIBANA – Love's Arrow – is a delightful posture, which gives deep and easy penetration and is very close and loving. He raises one of her feet up high, pressing it to his chest, her other leg stretched out straight.

By moving one of her feet the couple are in the posture known as VINASANA – the Lute – particularly adored by experienced women, says the poet of the *Ananga Ranga*. The penetration here is deeper and more intense.

To maintain the deep, close union, he can rock backwards and forwards, hardly moving his penis within her. This is a technique much in favour with the Tantrics and Taoists, said to be another of the infallible ways to engender love.

By twisting round onto her face from the previous position, she transforms it into the rear entry position EKABANDHA – the Knot. He kneels behind her with her hips pulled right back into his lap, giving very close intimacy, deep penetration and easy control…

*When a man, during congress, turns round, and enjoys the woman without leaving her, while she embraces him round the back all the time, it is called the 'turning position', and is learnt only by practice.*

By varying the angle at which he strikes in with his penis, he can massage her G-spot, the sensitive region which lies about two inches inside the vagina.

The *Kama Sutra* teaches that the degree of a lover's skill is determined by how far he or she can prolong the pleasure of making love. One way, when passion threatens to overwhelm you, is to regulate the rhythm of your breathing, with slow, deep breaths.

KIRTIBANDHA – the Famous Knot – is a relatively simple posture which cannot be bettered for deep, intimate penetration and just for being close. She sits astride his lap, her legs wrapped around his waist.

Lifting her knees up, with her weight on her feet and holding the headboard for support, this position is BHRAMARA – the Bee. It gives the woman complete control, allowing her to vary the direction, depth and rhythm of the penetration. Her swirling movements mimic those of a bee delving for pollen in a flower.

Then, by moving one foot to his chest, it becomes HANSA LILA – the Sporting of Swans. This opens her up more and enables her to send his penis almost anywhere she likes inside her pelvis.

Moving both feet to one side of him, and supporting herself if necessary on her elbows on his other side, we have HANSABANDHA – a second position

named for the Swan. This is not particularly easy to master, but gives a unique sensation as the angle of the penis and vagina diverge: another good position for finding the G-spot.

By resting the foot nearest his feet on one of his ankles, she reaches the GARUDA posture. This in turn can be twisted into PARAVRITTAKA – the Turnaround, in which she turns herself round to face his feet, reaches out and grasps them. This is a virtuoso move that can only be learned through practice. Not only does it afford deep and comfortable penetration but gives her lover a most erotic view of her buttocks repeatedly swallowing up his penis.

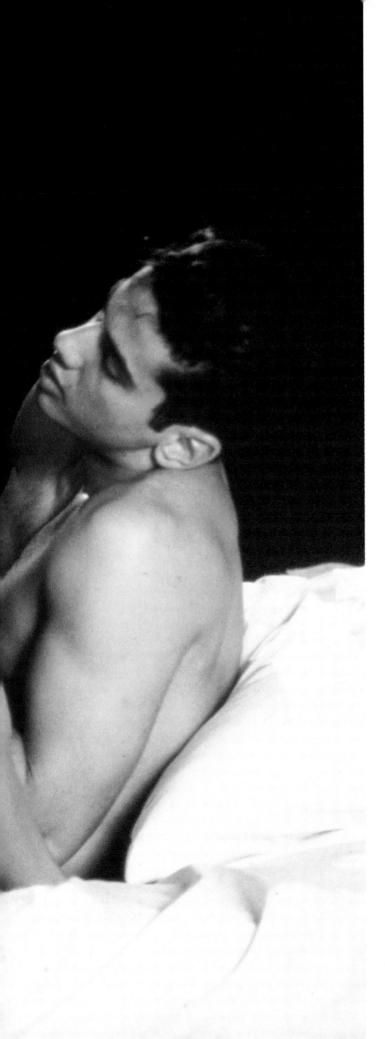

The signs of the enjoyment and satisfaction of the woman are as follows: her body relaxes, she closes her eyes, she puts aside all bashfulness, and shows increased willingness to unite the two organs as closely together as possible.

When lovers lie on a bed, and embrace each other so closely that the arms and thighs of the one are encircled by the arms and thighs of the other, and are, as it were, rubbing up against them, this is called an embrace like 'the mixture of sesamum seed with rice'.

When a man and a woman are very much in love with each other and, not thinking of any pain or hurt, embrace each other as if they were entering into each other's bodies, either while the woman is sitting on the lap of the man, or in front of him, or on a bed, then it is called an embrace like a 'mixture of milk and water'.

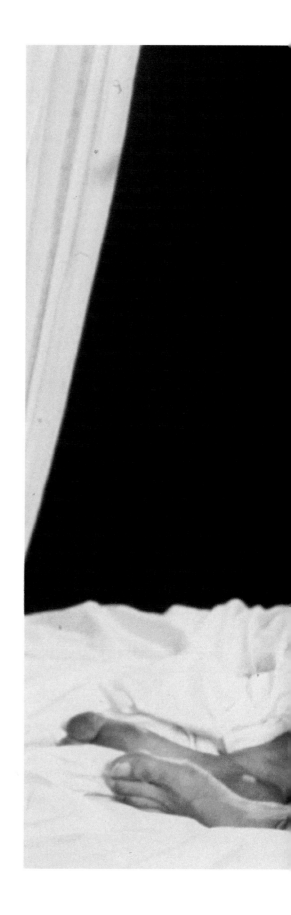

*Passionate actions and amorous gesticulations or movements, which arise on the spur of the moment, and during sexual intercourse, cannot be defined, and are as irregular as dreams. A horse having once attained the fifth degree of motion goes on with blind speed, regardless of pits, ditches, and posts in his way; and in the same manner a loving pair become blind with passion in the heat of congress, and go on with great impetuosity, paying not the least regard to excess. For this reason one who is well acquainted with the science of love, and knowing his own strength, as also the tenderness, impetuosity and strength of the young woman, should act accordingly.*

There will be times when passion creeps up on you when you are least expecting it and is so overwhelming that it cannot be denied.

Acting impetuously, on the spur of the moment, can, it would seem, be as inconvenient as it is exciting, so it is a good idea to know a few techniques that will be useful when, like lightning, passion strikes.

*Of all the lovers of a girl, he only is her true husband*
*who possesses the qualities that are liked by her,*
*and such a husband only enjoys real superiority*
*over her, because he is the husband of love.*

*Whatever things may be done by one
of the lovers to the other, the same
should be returned... if the woman
kisses him he should kiss her in return.*

The energy flows in a circuit
within the body of each
lover. But when their lips
and tongues and their teeth
make contact, when they
indulge in the beautiful kiss
that the *Kama Sutra* calls
'the fighting of tongues',
then their two love circuits
become one, the energy
flowing from body to body.

When a girl only touches the mouth of her lover with
her own, but does not herself do anything,
it is called the 'nominal kiss'.

When a girl, setting aside her bashfulness a little,
wishes to touch the lip that is pressed into her mouth,
and with that object moves her lower lip, but not the
upper one, it is called the 'throbbing kiss'.

When a girl touches her lover's lip with her tongue,
and having shut her eyes, places her hands on those of
her lover, it is called the 'touching kiss'.

When the lips of two lovers and brought into direct
contact with each other, it is called a 'straight kiss'.

When the heads of two lovers are bent towards each
other, and when so bent, kissing takes place,
it is called a 'bent kiss'.

When one of them turns up the face of the other by
holding the head and chin, and then kissing,
it is called a 'turned kiss'.

Lastly, when the lower lip is pressed with much force,
it is called a 'pressed kiss'.

*Acts to be done by the man:*

*When the organs are brought together properly and directly it is called 'moving the organ forward'.*

*When the lingam is held with the hand, and turned all round in the yoni, it is called 'churning'.*

*When the yoni is lowered and the upper part of it is struck with the lingam, it is called 'piercing'.*

*When the same thing is done on the lower part of the yoni, it is called 'rubbing'.*

*When the yoni is pressed by the lingam for a long time, it is called 'pressing'*

*When both sides of the yoni are rubbed in this way, it is called the 'blow of a bull'.*

If she enjoys it, he may try withdrawing completely, and then striking in, hard, to the full length of his penis. This is called NIRGHATA – the Buffet. It can be varied by her slightly crossing her legs and placing both heels on one of his shoulders, an elegant posture which enables him to keep up the pressure against one wall of her vagina. This is VARAHAGHATA – the Boar's Thrust.

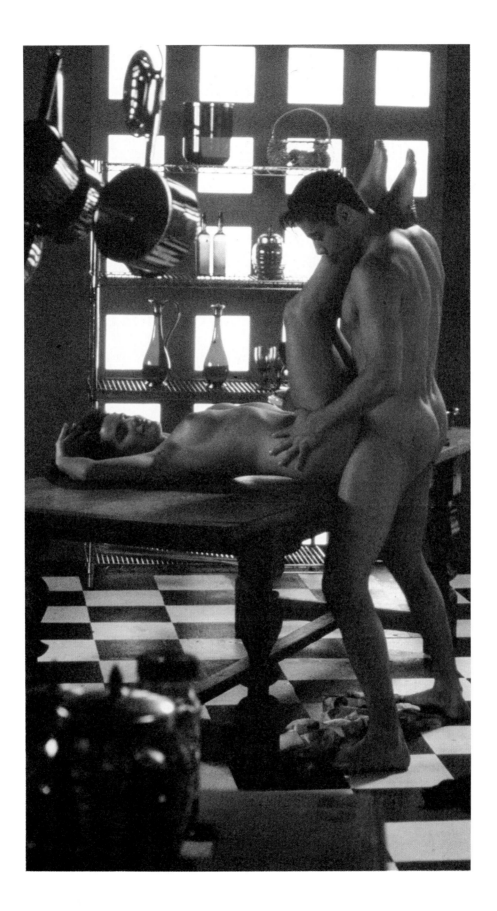

Boisterous lovemaking, especially when using a hard table instead of soft cushions, can sometimes cause bumps and bruises. But as Vatsyayana observes, when we are alone and see again the marks of passion on our bodies, feelings of love come welling up afresh.

Sitting on the very edge of the table with her heels on the rim and with her arms locked around his neck gives a position that affords very deep penetration. As this may be a little uncomfortable for her, in order to press in closely and delay ejaculation he may hold his penis pressed breathlessly in as deep as it will go. This technique is known as PIDITAKA – Pressing.

From this position she locks her legs completely around his waist and he lifts her off completely, converting the posture to a standing one. Known as AVALAMBITAKA – Suspended, this is a simple move to get into, but one that can be quite difficult to hold for long.

Sitting on the chair, he disengages her feet from
behind his back and puts her feet on the ground –
using the leverage to control the depth, speed and
direction of his thrusts.

This sequence of postures, if done seated on the
floor, would be attainable only by yoga students.

DOLITA – the Swing. Using the leverage of her
feet, she swings her hips around.

KSHUDGARA – the Striking. Lifting her feet up
a little, she increases the depth and angle of his penis
within her, while still retaining complete control
of her own movements.

By lifting her feet to the sides of the
chair she is completely opened up to
him and yet still able to do exactly
as she likes with the penis. She may
vary the rhythm and depth of her
thrusts down on him. Five shallow
and one deep thrust, for instance,
is a technique much praised
by Taoists.

*Acts to be done by the woman:*

*When the woman holds the lingam in her yoni, draws it in, presses it, and keeps it thus in her for a long time, it is called the 'pair of tongs'.*

*When, while engaged in congress, she turns round like a wheel, it is called the 'top'. This is learnt by practice only.*

*When the woman is tired, she should place her forehead on that of her lover, and should thus take rest without disturbing the union of the organs, and when the woman has rested herself the man should turn round and begin the congress again.*

Turning her back to him sheaths the penis deeply in her vagina. She can now use her muscles to grip and squeeze it. If she takes his penis within her to its full length, then squeezes hard as she very slowly lets it withdraw, as though 'milking' it with her vagina, then it is known as VADAVAKA – the Mare, which is only learned by practice. Yet any woman *can* learn it, if she is willing to practise squeezing and relaxing the muscles of her vagina one hundred times a day.

*In the garden... plant beds of green vegetables,*
*bunches of the sugar cane, and clumps of the fig tree,*
*the mustard plant, the parsley plant and the fennel*
*plant. Clusters of various flowers such as the wild*
*jasmine, the yellow amaranth, Arabian and*
*Spanish jasmines, the frangipani, and the fragrant*
*white flower called Queen of the Night should*
*likewise be planted, together with flowering groves*
*of Indian coral and catechu trees, banana palms*
*and tall strands of fresh-smelling khus knus grass.*
*Footpaths should lead from the house and wander*
*between the flowers and trees. In the garden*
*there should also be a whirling swing and a*
*common swing, as also a bower of creepers covered*
*with flowers, in which a raised parterre should be*
*made for sitting.*

The ideal garden for the third century citizen
was a place to relax, and a place to make love
in. If you are lucky enough to have a garden of your
own, private and not overlooked, you can use it to
enhance your own lovemaking.

*Kissing is of four kinds...moderate, contracted,
pressed, and soft, according to the different parts
of the body which are kissed.*

The objective of the postures
and techniques advocated by the
*Kama Sutra* is not to acquire
virtuosity but to build love between
husband and wife

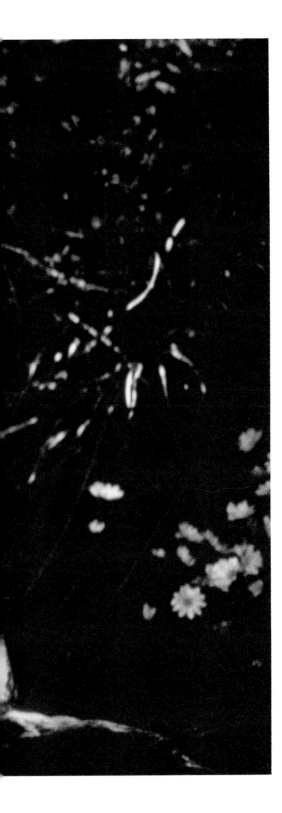

Four mouths are pure, says the *Kama Sutra*: the mouth of a sucking calf, the mouth of a hunting dog seizing its quarry, a bird's beak severing fruit from trees, and the mouth of a woman during lovemaking.

When performing fellatio the woman has many subtle little techniques to give him pleasure.

*When, holding the man's lingam with her hand, and
placing it between her lips, the woman moves about her
mouth, it is called the 'nominal congress'.*

When, covering the end of the lingam with her fingers
collected together like the bud of a plant or flower, the
woman presses the sides of it with her lips, using her
teeth also, it is called 'biting the sides'.

When the woman presses the end of the lingam with her
lips closed together, and kisses it as if she were drawing
it out, it is called the 'outside pressing'.

When she puts the lingam further into her mouth, and
presses it with her lips and then takes it out, it is called
the 'inside pressing'.

When, holding the lingam in her hand, the woman
kisses it as if she were kissing the lower lip,
it is called 'kissing'.

When, after kissing it, she touches it with her tongue
everywhere, and passes the tongue over the end of it, it
is called 'rubbing'.

When, in the same way, she puts the half of it into her
mouth, and forcibly kisses and sucks it, this is called
'sucking a mango'.

And lastly, when the woman puts the whole lingam
into her mouth, and presses it to the very end, as if
she were going to swallow it up, it is called
'swallowing up'.

She straddles him so he can lick at her clitoris while
she continues to fellate him. This is the famous
soixante-neuf, known in Indian tradition as
KAKILA – the Lovemaking of the Crow.

Given that the tradition recognises eight
techniques of fellatio and eight of cunnilingus, it
means that there are at least 64 ways in which
to enjoy '69'.

In this embrace he supports her
knees with his elbows: this posture is
known as J A N U K U R P A R A —
Knee Elbow

The *Kama Sutra*, and all the Indian love texts that
followed it, always reserved a special pride of place for
the standing postures, which were thought difficult
and therefore especially splendid. They were called
'picture positions' because these were the postures
chosen by sculptors to adorn temple walls.

GARDHABA – the Ass
– is a very close,
intimate way of
coupling, giving
intense pleasure to
both partners. She
stands with her back to
him, he bends his knees
and takes her from
behind. This is a
position which can be
seen on the walls
of many Khajuraho
temples.

*An ingenious person should multiply the kinds of
congress after the fashion of the different kinds of beasts
and birds. For these different kinds of congress,
performed according to the usage of each country, and
the liking of the individual, generate love, friendship
and respect in the hearts of women.*

TALA – the Palm.
Lifting one foot up high
in his palm opens her
up wide to him. This
sensual and beautiful
posture can also easily
be performed using
a chair.

Pushing her feet against
the tree trunk, she can
make the transition into
AVALAMBITAKA
– Suspended, which
enables her to rock her
hips back and forth
against him.

When a man and a woman support themselves on each others bodies, or on a wall, or pillar, and thus while standing engage in congress, it is called the 'supported congress'.

When a man supports himself against a wall, and the woman, sitting on his hands joined together and held underneath her, throws her arms round his neck, and putting her thighs alongside his waist, moves herself by her feet, which are touching the wall against which the man is leaning, it is called the 'suspended congress'.

When a woman stands on her hands and feet like a quadruped, and her lover mounts her like a bull, it is called the 'congress of a cow'. At this time everything that is ordinarily done on the bosom should be done on the back.

In the same way can be carried on the congress of a dog, the congress of a goat, the congress of a deer, the forcible mounting of an ass, the congress of a cat, the jump of a tiger, the pressing of an elephant, the rubbing of a boar, and the mounting of a horse.

TRIPADAM — the
Tripod. Letting her foot
drop down he catches
her knee, ending up
with three feet on the
ground.

*When a woman, clinging to a man as a creeper
twines round a tree, bends his head down to hers
with the desire of kissing him and slightly makes
the sound of sut sut, embraces him, and looks
lovingly towards him, it is called an embrace like
the 'twining of a creeper'.*

*When a woman, having placed one of her feet on
the foot of her lover, and the other on one of his
thighs, passes one of her arms round his back,
and the other on his shoulders, makes slightly the
sounds of singing and cooing, and wishes, as it
were, to climb up him in order to have a kiss, it is
called an embrace like the 'climbing of a tree'.*

*These two kinds of embrace take place when the
lover is standing.*

For the ancient Indians, lovemaking
went beyond the merely human
and mortal. It touched the divine
itself. No coincidence perhaps that
a story that began with a god and
goddess locked away in a ten
thousand year passion should end
with a posture dedicated to another
god: for this lovely, natural position
is called TRAIVIKRAMA, the Stride
of Vishnu, after the god Vishnu who
covered the earth in three strides.

Vatsyayana concluded the *Kama Sutra* with the following flourish:

*A man, employing the sixty-four means mentioned by Babhravya, obtains his object, and enjoys the woman of the first quality. Though he may speak well on other subjects, if he does not know the sixty-four divisions, no great respect is paid to him in the assembly of the learned. A man, devoid of other knowledge, but well acquainted with the sixty-four divisions, becomes a leader in any society of men and women. . . As the sixty-four arts are respected, are charming, and add to the talent of women, they are called by the Acharyas dear to women.*

Richard Burton, sensing perhaps that the lengthy work he had laboured over for so long was to become known as one of the world's great books, ended his translation with Shakespeare's moving elegiac couplet:

*So long as lips shall kiss, and eyes shall see,*
*So long lives This, and This gives life to Thee.*

M
any more sexual positions and techniques are described in The *Perfumed Garden*, another classic work on lovemaking from the ancient East. Originally written by Sheikh Nefzawi, this too was translated by Richard Burton. We have included a selection here, as they admirably complement those in the *Kama Sutra*.

*Concerning the Different Postures for Coition*
The ways of uniting with a woman are numerous and varied, and the time has arrived when you should learn the different postures. God has said: 'Woman is your field, go to your field with a will!' (*Koran*). According to your taste you may choose the posture which

pleases you most, provided always that intercourse takes place through the appointed organ: the yoni.

FIRST POSTURE: Lay the woman on her back and raise her thighs; then, getting between her legs, introduce your lingam. Gripping the ground with your toes, you will be able to move in a suitable manner. This posture is a good one for those who have long members.

SECOND POSTURE: If your lingam is short, lay the woman on her back and raise her legs in the air so that her toes touch her ears. Her buttocks being thus raised, the yoni is thrown forward. Now introduce your lingam.

THIRD POSTURE: Lay the woman on the ground and get between her thighs; then, putting one of her legs on your shoulder and the other under your arm, penetrate her.

FOURTH POSTURE: Stretch the woman on the ground and put her legs on your shoulders; in that position your lingam will be exactly opposite her yoni which will be lifted off the ground. That is the moment for introducing your lingam.

FIFTH POSTURE: Let the woman lie on her side on the ground; then, lying down yourself and getting between her thighs, introduce your lingam. This posture is apt to give rise to rheumatic or sciatic pains.

SIXTH POSTURE: Let the woman rest on her knees and elbows in the position for prayer. In this posture the yoni stands out behind.

SEVENTH POSTURE: Lay the woman on her side, and then you yourself sitting on your heels will place her top leg on your nearest shoulder and her other leg against your thighs. She will keep on her side and you will be between her legs. Introduce your lingam and move her backwards and forwards with your hands.

EIGHTH POSTURE: Lay the woman on her back and kneel astride her.

NINTH POSTURE: Place the woman so that she rests, either face forward or the reverse, against a slightly raised platform, her feet remaining on the ground and her body projecting in front. She will thus present her yoni to your lingam which you will introduce.

TENTH POSTURE: Place the woman on a rather low divan and let her grasp the woodwork with her hands. Then, placing her legs on your hips and telling her to grip your body with them, you will introduce your lingam, at the same time grasping the divan. When you begin to work, let your movements keep time.

ELEVENTH POSTURE: Lay the woman on her back and let her buttocks be raised by a cushion placed under them. Let her put the soles of her feet together: now get between her thighs.

There are other postures besides the preceding in use in India. It is well that you should know that the Hindus have greatly multiplied the ways of possessing a woman and have carried their investigations in this matter much further than the Arabs. Among other postures and variations are the following:

THE CLOSURE: Lay the woman on her back and raise her buttocks with a cushion; then get between her legs, keeping your toes on the floor, and force her thighs against her chest. Now pass your hands under her arms to clasp her to you, or tightly grip her shoulders. That done, introduce your lingam and draw her towards you at the moment of ejaculation. This posture is painful for the woman, for, with her thighs pressed on her chest and her buttocks raised with the cushion, the walls of the vagina are forced together, and, as a consequence – the uterus being pushed forward – there is not enough room for the lingam which can only be inserted with difficulty, and which impinges on the womb. This posture should only be used when the lingam is short and soft.

THE FROG'S POSTURE: Place the woman on her back and raise her thighs till her heels are close to her buttocks. Now seat yourself in front of her yoni and introduce your lingam; then put her knees under your armpits and, grasping the upper part of her arms, draw her to you at the propitious moment.

THE CLASPING OF HANDS AND FEET: Lay the woman on her back, then sit on your heels between her thighs and grip the floor with your toes; she will now put her legs round your body and you will put your arms about her neck.

THE RAISED LEGS POSTURE: While the woman is lying on her back take hold of her legs and, holding them close together, raise them until her soles point to the ceiling; then clasping her between your thighs, introduce your lingam, taking care at the same time not to let her legs fall.

THE GOAT'S POSTURE: Let the woman lie on her side and stretch out her bottom leg. Crouch down between her thighs, lift her top leg and introduce your lingam. Hold her by the arms or shoulders.

THE ARCHIMEDEAN SCREW: While the man is lying on his back the woman sits on his lingam, keeping her face towards his. She then places her hands on the bed, at the same time keeping her belly off his; she now moves up and down and, if the man is light in weight, he may move as well. If the woman wishes to kiss the man she need only lay her arms on the bed.

THE SOMERSAULT: The woman should let her trousers fall to her ankles so that they are like fetters. She then bends down till her head is in her trousers, when the man, seizing her legs, pulls her over onto her back. He then kneels down and penetrates her. It is said that there are women, who, when lying on their back, can put their feet under their head without the help of their hands or trousers.

THE OSTRICH'S TAIL: Lay the woman on the ground and kneel at her feet; then raise her legs and place them round your neck so that only her head and shoulders remain on the ground. Now penetrate her.

PUTTING ON THE SOCK: The woman being on her back, you sit between her legs and place your lingam between the lips of her yoni which you grasp with the thumb and first finger. You then move so that the part of your lingam which is in contact with the woman is subjected to rubbing, and continue so until her yoni is moist with the liquid which escapes from your penis. Having thus given her a foretaste of pleasure, you penetrate her completely.

THE MUTUAL VIEW OF THE BUTTOCKS: The man lies on his back, and the woman, turning her back to him, sits on his lingam. He now clasps her body with his legs and she leans over until her hands touch the floor. Thus supported she has a view of his buttocks, and he of hers, and she is able to move conveniently.

DRAWING THE BOW: Let the woman lie on her side, and the man, also on his side, gets between her legs so that his face is turned towards her back; now, placing his hands on her shoulders, he introduces

his lingam. The woman then grasps the man's feet and draws them towards her; she forms thus, with the man's body, a bow to which she is the arrow.

RECIPROCATING MOTION: The man, seated on the ground, brings the soles of his feet together, at the same time lowering his thighs. The woman then sits on his feet and clasps his body with her legs and his neck with her arms. The man then grasps the woman's legs, and, moving his feet towards his body, carries the woman within reach of his lingam, which he introduces. By a movement of his feet he now moves her backwards and forwards. The woman should take care to facilitate this movement by not pressing too heavily. If the man fears that his lingam will be drawn right out, he must grasp the woman round the body and be satisfied with such movement as he can give with his feet.

POUNDING THE SPOT: The man sits down and stretches out his legs, and the woman sits on his thighs and crosses her legs behind his back. She places her yoni opposite his lingam and lends a guiding hand. She then puts her arms round his neck, and he puts his round her waist and raises and lowers her on his lingam, in which movement she assists.

COITION FROM BEHIND: The woman lies face downwards and raises her buttocks with a cushion; the man lies on her back and introduces his lingam

while she slips her arms through his elbows.

BELLY TO BELLY: The man and the woman stand face to face, the latter with her feet slightly apart, the man's feet being between. Both now advance their feet. The man should now place one foot in advance of the other, and each should clasp the other round the loins. The man then penetrates and both move in the manner explained later on. (See FIRST MOVEMENT.)

THE SHEEP'S POSTURE: The woman kneels down and puts her forearms on the ground; the man kneels down behind her and slips his lingam in her yoni which she makes stand out as much as possible. His hands should be placed on her shoulders.

THE CAMEL'S HUMP: The woman, who is standing, bends forward till her fingers touch the floor; the man gets behind and copulates, at the same time grasping her thighs. If the man withdraws while the woman is still bending down, the yoni emits a sound like the bleating of a calf, and for that reason women object to the posture.

DRIVING IN THE PEG: While facing each other, the woman, hanging with her arms round the man's neck, raises her legs and with them clasps him round the waist, resting her feet against a wall. The man now introduces his lingam, and the woman is then as if hanging on a peg.

THE FUSION OF LOVE: The woman lies on her

right side and you on your left; stretch your bottom leg straight down and raise your other leg, letting it rest on the woman's side. Now pull the woman's top leg onto your body and then introduce your lingam. The woman may help if she likes, to make the necessary movements.

INVERSION: The man lies on his back and the woman lies on him. She grasps his thighs and draws them towards her, thus bringing his lingam into prominence. Having guided it in, she puts her hands on the bed, one on each side of the man's buttocks. It is necessary for her feet to be raised on a cushion to allow for the slope of the lingam. The woman moves. This posture may be varied by the woman sitting on her heels between the man's legs.

RIDING THE LINGAM: The man lies down and places a cushion under his shoulders, taking care that his buttocks remain on the floor. Thus placed, he raises his legs till his knees are close to his face. The woman then sits on his lingam. She does not lie down, but sits astride, as though on a saddle formed by the man's legs and chest. By bending her knees she can now move upwards and downwards; or, she may put her knees on the floor, in which case the man moves her with his thighs while she grasps his shoulders.

THE JOINTER: The man and the woman sit down facing each other; the woman then puts her right

thigh on the man's left thigh, and he puts his right thigh on her left one. The woman guides his lingam into her yoni and grasps the man's arms while he grasps hers. They now indulge in a see-saw motion, leaning backwards and forwards alternately, taking care that their movements are well-timed.

THE STAY-AT-HOME: The woman lies on her back, and the man, with cushions under his hands, lies on her. When the introduction has taken place the woman raises her buttocks as far as possible from the bed, and the man accompanies her in the movement, taking care that his lingam is not withdrawn. The woman then drops her buttocks with short sharp jerks, and, although the two are not clasped together, the man should keep quite close to the woman. They continue this movement, but it is necessary that the man be light and the bed soft; otherwise pain will be caused.

THE BLACKSMITH'S POSTURE: The woman lies on her back with a cushion under her buttocks. She draws her knees onto her chest so that her yoni stands out like a sieve; she then guides in the lingam. The man now performs for a moment or two the conventional movements. He then withdraws his lingam and slips it between the women's thighs in imitation of the blacksmith who draws the hot iron from the fire and plunges it into cold water.

THE SEDUCTIVE POSTURE: The woman lies on her back and the man crouches between her legs which he then puts under his arms or on his shoulders. He may hold her by the waist or the arms.

I have not thought it necessary to mention those postures which appeared to me impossible of accomplishment and, if anyone should think the number given is too small, he has nothing to do but invent more. It is incontestable that the Hindus have surmounted enormous difficulties in postures for coition; the following is an example: the woman lies on her back and the man sits astride her chest, facing towards her feet. He now bends forward and raises her thighs till her yoni is opposite his lingam which he then introduces. As you can see, this posture is diffi-

cult to execute and very tiring. I think it is only realisable in thought or design.

It is related that there are women who, during coition, can raise one of their legs in the air and balance a lighted lamp on the sole of their foot, without spilling the oil or extinguishing the lamp. Intercourse is not interfered with by this action which demands, however, great skill. Nevertheless, the things to be sought for most in copulation, those which give the greatest pleasure, are the embraces, the kisses, and the sucking of each other's lips. These differentiate man from the animals. No one is insensible to the pleasures which arise from difference of sex, and man's highest pleasure is copulation. When a man's love is carried to its highest pitch, all the pleasures of coition become easy for him, and he satisfies them by embracing and kissing. There is the real source of happiness for both.

It is advisable that the connoisseur of copulation should try all the postures so that he may know which gives pleasure to the woman. He will then adopt that for preference and will have the satisfaction of retaining the woman's affection. By universal consent, *pounding on the spot* gives most satisfaction.

It remains now for me to speak of the different movements used in copulation.

FIRST MOVEMENT: The Bucket in the Well. The man and woman embrace closely after penetration, then the man moves once and slightly draws back; the woman now moves and withdraws in her turn, and so on alternately. They should take care to place their hands and feet against each other's and imitate, as well as they can, the descent of a bucket in a well.

SECOND MOVEMENT: The Mutual Shock. Both draw away after the introduction, taking care that the lingam is not entirely withdrawn; they then come together smartly and closely embrace. They continue thus.

THIRD MOVEMENT: Going Shares. The man moves in the usual manner, then stops; the woman, keeping the lingam in place, moves once, then stops. The man now recommences, and so they continue till they ejaculate.

FOURTH MOVEMENT: Love's Tailor. The man partly penetrates and moves with a rubbing motion; then, with a single stroke, he enters completely. Such is the action of a tailor who, after having inserted his needle, draws it through with a single pull. This movement is only suitable for those who can control their ejaculation.

FIFTH MOVEMENT: The Toothpick. The man introduces his lingam and explores the yoni from top to bottom and on all sides.

SIXTH MOVEMENT: Love's Bond. The man penetrates completely so that his body is perfectly close to the woman's. He should now move energetically, taking care that not the smallest portion is withdrawn from the yoni. This is the best movement of all, and it is particularly suitable for pounding the spot. Women prefer it to the exclusion of all others as it procures them the greatest pleasure, and allows the yoni to clasp the lingam. Tribads use no other movement, and it can be recommended to all who suffer from a premature ejaculation.

Any posture is unsatisfactory if kissing is impossible; pleasure will be incomplete, for a kiss is one of the most potent stimulants of all.

It is claimed by some that kissing is an integral part of copulation. The most delightful kiss is that which is planted on moist ardent lips, and accompanied with suction of the lips and tongue, so that the emission of a sweet intoxicating saliva is produced. It is for the man to procure this emission from the woman by gently nibbling her lips and tongue till she secretes a particular saliva, sweet, exquisite, more agreeable than honey mixed with pure water, and which does not mix with her ordinary saliva. This gives the man a shivering sensation throughout his whole body, and is more intoxicating than strong wine. A kiss should be sonorous. Its sound, light and prolonged, takes its rise between the tongue and the moist edge of the palate. It is produced by a movement of the tongue in the mouth and a displacement of the saliva provoked by suction. A kiss given on the outside of the lips and accompanied with a sound like that made when calling a cat, gives no pleasure whatever. Such a kiss is only meant for children, or the hands. The kiss which I have described above, and which belongs to copulation, provokes a delicious voluptuousness. It is for you to learn the difference.

"Love has many yogas:
the touching of two bodies; the locking of groins;
the drawing apart in separation;
the quieting of the violent breath;
the still release from body and mind...
The wise know that physical pleasure
is not the sole end of lovemaking.
It can be like music, stirring the emotions,
quickening the senses, dissolving
thought into rhythm, until only rhythm exists.
On and on it flows as hearts thud faster,
limbs tremble in the beat
of drums that double pace and double again,
till that music itself breaks
into one long holy note of silence."

## BIBLIOGRAPHY

It has not been possible in this edition to include the entire text of the *Kama Sutra*. However, the following editions are recommended:

*The Kama Sutra*, edited by WG Archer, Allen & Unwin 1965, Aquarian Press 1991

*The Kama Sutra of Vatsyayana*, edited by John Muirhead-Gould with an introduction by Dom Moraes, Grafton Books 1963

*The Love Teachings of Kama Sutra*, trans. Indra Sinha, Hamlyn 1980

*The Illustrated Kama Sutra, Ananga Ranga, Perfumed Garden*, edited by Charles Fowkes, Hamlyn 1987